LAST ORDERS

Before You Go

A book for the living
The ultimate guide to dying happy

KATHIE SHEARER

RP

RYAN
PUBLISHING

First published 2025 by Ryan Publishing
PO Box 7680, Melbourne, 3004
Victoria, Australia
Ph: 61 3 9505 6820
Email: books@ryanpub.com
Website: www.ryanpub.com

A catalogue record for this
book is available from the
National Library of Australia

Last Orders
Before You Go

Paperback: 9781876498818

Internal and cover design by Luke Harris, Working Type Studio,
Victoria, Australia. www.workingtype.com.au
Edited by Martin Blake

The Shearer lads whom
I love more than life:
Bobby, Brett and Jake

FOREWORD
BY MIKE CLAYTON

*Golf course designer, published writer
and professional golfer*

My first memory of Kathie Shearer was way back in 1974 at Royal Melbourne Golf Club. We'd all read about Bob Shearer's English girlfriend, but there's nothing like a first sighting.

Bob was, for my generation, the hero of every golf-obsessed kid in Melbourne and here was our man walking off the 54th green with a seven-shot lead in the Chrysler Classic and his arm around one of the most astonishing looking women any of us had ever seen. Does life, I thought, get any better?

Half a dozen years later I'd turned pro and met

Bob and, by association, Kathie who in the late 1980s became the staple organiser of golf tournament media centres across the country. She ran them with the iron-fist of someone who'd grown up a tough, east-end Londoner who never took a backward step and was fiercely loyal to anyone on her side. No one messed with Kathie, the press writers all knew her rules and so long as everyone played along, the operation ran like clockwork.

A couple of years after Bob won at Royal Melbourne, a big, blond kid from Queensland won his first tournament, The West Lakes Classic, in Adelaide.

Greg Norman was, and remains, the biggest-ever Australian golf star with an extraordinary charisma and a great ability to write the following morning's headlines by throwing the writers something controversial.

He could also be prickly if he'd had an annoying finish to his day or his week but no matter his position in the tournament the journalists wanted to speak with him. No one understood how to manage Greg quite like Kathie, who'd be watching the leader boards to see if she could send one of the underlings to the back of the 18th green to "get Greg" and bring him to a quizzing by the golf writers. A good day and he'd be in a good mood, but a not so good one and Kathie knew she was the only one for the job. No matter how annoyed he might have been, Greg Norman never said no to Kathie Shearer.

Nor did Tiger Woods.

At the 1998 Johnnie Walker Classic in Thailand, Tiger was the star, and when you're the biggest sports star in the world you get to make the rules.

The incident was all over his manager from IMG, "Clark Jones or Clark Kent or whatever his name was."

Unknown to Kathie, Tiger's deal was that if he wasn't in the first three on the leaderboard, he didn't have to talk to the media.

After shooting rounds of 72 and 71, he was miles off the half-way pace, but Kathie found Tiger in the locker room and said, "Look, you really need to come in."

To which Tiger replied with, "I don't fucking have to."

The IMG man, Tiger's manager, according to Kathie, "butted in when I was having this conversation and kept repeating the same thing – which tipped me over the edge"

"Listen", said Kathie, "I'm talking to the butcher not the block. You can fuck off."

With that Tiger dutifully hopped into a golf cart and accompanied Kathie to the media centre.

"From that day onwards he's been as good as gold. Fantastic, he hasn't carried a grudge at all."

Not so long after, at the 1998 Presidents Cup at Royal Melbourne, Bob was introduced to Tiger.

"Are you related to Kathie Shearer?"

"Yes, I'm married to her."

"Well," said Tiger, "You're a hell of a man."

Of course, Kathie is much more than golf. Her two boys, Bobbie and Brett, could not ask for a better protector. She looked after her mum, who followed her to Australia and lived the rest of her long life in Melbourne. When Bob was away playing or later travelling with his golf course design work, it was Kathie who held the whole show together.

Twenty years ago, Kathie added becoming a Celebrant to her life's wide experience, and with all the insights which end-of-life celebrations gave her, she has turned her attention to this wise and heartfelt book.

Her advice was invaluable to me when my mother died while I was overseas, leaving my wife to deal with some extremely challenging circumstances. There could have been no better person to have in our corner than Kathie. With this book, you too can have her in your corner. I couldn't recommend a kinder, better or safer pair of hands.

That long-ago 1974 sighting at Royal Melbourne was of an astonishing looking woman.

Half a century later it's been my privilege to know, and write this foreword, for a truly astonishing woman.

When we are born, the world rejoices and we cry.
When we die, the world cries and we rejoice.

Native American proverb

CONTENTS

Welcome to *Last Orders*, the only book you will ever need to put your wishes, aspirations, memories and other affairs in order before you depart this wonderful world to life everlasting, or wherever your beliefs take you.

My name is Kathie Shearer and I have written this book to help you navigate through the complicated maze of dying while you are still alive and kicking. I have drawn on my own life lessons, from growing up in a depressed post-war London, experiencing a massive family tragedy aged 12, and working as a marriage and funeral celebrant for 17 years in Melbourne, Australia.

It's a difficult topic which I've addressed seriously, but also with a smile, which is important. Two of the biggest influences and pleasures in my life are music and laughter so I have included references to my favourite song titles, sayings and proverbs at every opportunity. I hope they resonate with you, and make you smile too.

This book is here to lighten the load when it comes to the heavy subject of death (and I should add that this term, 'death', will be used sparingly from now on as this is a book for the living). We are diving into the deep end of this taboo subject with a chuckle.

You see, just like planning a wedding (minus the cake-tasting and bridal fittings), a birthday party (minus the birthday boy or girl), it's quite considerate to sort out your exit strategy ahead of time. After all, who wants to leave their loved ones drowning in paperwork and guesswork when they are already grieving?

Think of it like taking the reins of your destiny while you are still in control.

I stumbled upon this idea over a casual chat, possibly fuelled by a few glasses of the good stuff rather than coffee, to be totally honest.

So, I thought, "why not demystify the whole shebang? Let's break down the nitty-gritty of what happens after we kick the bucket in a way that's as easy as a Sunday morning."

Indeed, we are talking about everything from dividing up your money to deciding who gets

Grandma's collection of porcelain cats. Because let's face it, everyone's idea of a good time is different. Some might want to blow it all on a world tour, while others might want to leave a legacy for their furry friends or a favourite cause.

Now, I know what you are thinking. Talking about death with a wink and a nod might seem a tad irreverent, even inappropriate. But let's call it how it is. Death is going to happen, whether we are ready or not, and being prepared is the name of the game.

Wouldn't this time be a lot easier if your nearest and dearest knew exactly what you wanted, without having to play a game of psychic detective? That's where *Last Orders* comes in handy. It's like having a GPS for the afterlife.

We are not reinventing the wheel; we are just making sure that it rolls smoothly when the time comes. Think wills, power of attorney, funeral requests – the whole nine yards. It might sound daunting, but it does not need to be. Together with this easy-to-read book, I have produced a step-by-step tutorial that's easier to follow than a recipe for microwave popcorn.

Now, you might be thinking, isn't this a bit

morbid? A very fair point, but hear me out. In my experience, there is something oddly comforting about knowing you have your ducks in a row, even when the end seems light-years away.

And we are not here to rain on anyone's parade, whether you're a devout believer or a sceptic. *Last Orders* is all about options. It's your life (and death), after all, and what you do about this is entirely up to you.

Everyone knows that life is too short for squabbles over who gets Great Aunt Mildred's teapot collection. It makes total sense to take control, crack open *Last Orders*, and ride off into the sunset knowing that you do have things covered – from cradle to grave, and every chuckle in between.

Now let me take your hand so we can take this journey together.

*   *   *

Spaces have been set aside through the book to record love notes, details and contact information to help with your planning.

1. WHY SHOULD YOU LISTEN TO ME, I HEAR YOU SAY?

I have lived for two my whole life,
double shots of everything.
– Kathie Shearer (2025)

My own journey through life has taken me from hawker in a London street market, a wig model, corporate media assistant, a professional golfer's wife, long-standing golf media professional, public speaker, experienced celebrant and now to my next chapter, writing this book.

All my life, an abundance of stories have been sitting in the corridors of my mind and struggling to escape. My earliest memories date to London as a little girl, stemming and wiring flowers with my cousins at my Nan's flower shop on Roman Road, when it was all hands on deck (including the little ones) for the big East End funerals.

Indulge me, if you will, as I share some of these stories. My hope is that they will help, inform, comfort and/or make you smile as you begin to plan your final big event.

I was born on the 29th of January 1951 in the Royal London Hospital in Whitechapel, in London's East End, within earshot of the famous Bow Bells of St Mary-le-Bow church. I therefore qualify as a 24-carat gold Cockney as well as a very proud and indigenous Londoner. Coincidentally my Mum was born in the same hospital, on the same date, possibly at the same time and possibly in the same room, exactly 30 years previously, as the family folklore goes.

My mother carried me as a twin, but she miscarried my sibling at four months. It was more than 70 years ago, and neither my mother nor the doctors knew that she was carrying twins initially. Mum told me much later that she knew she was still carrying a child, even after the miscarriage. Everyone thought it was a phantom pregnancy, but the phantom was me!

I had a lovely childhood. I always felt wanted, but my mother Bette Melvin was the boss and her sister Jane (who we called Jinny) was just as formidable. Bruce Springsteen was an amateur 'boss' compared to those two.

Any sniff of trouble (particularly related to monies owed) and these two formidable women – unasked – would put on their coats, hats and gloves and go to see what the problem was. To my knowledge, everything would be resolved with no fuss (debt paid in full) or at least that's what I was told

I came from a hard-working East End family. By day my Nan, Aunties, Mum and even my Dad ran a very successful florist shop in Bethnal Green Road, specialising in catering for those huge funerals which were the custom in those days.

We stuck together, as East Enders did. As my mum always said, "Get up, dress up and show up."

To be brutally honest, this working arrangement, as we say in London, was not Dad's 'cup of tea'. His job was to manually transport heavy wooden cases of flowers on a large barrow from our warehouse to the shop, often with me sitting on top. He always called me his flying angel.

Sometimes there would be a detour into a local public house called the Rising Sun, conveniently located between the warehouse and the flower shop. I could often be seen sitting with the other kids on the front step of the pub drinking a top shelf Britvic pineapple juice with a bag of unflavoured crisps with a blue salt bag enclosed. That was, of course, until my Mum came looking.

As for those funerals, the biggest fear was 'the nine o'clock trot'. Anytime a funeral was held before nine o'clock you knew that the families were poor and could not afford a proper send-off. It was customary at that time for families to pay a weekly amount to an insurance company to cover funeral costs, normally a penny a week.

This custom was widespread and was a forerunner to what we now consider the pre-paid funeral. People were terrified of being buried in an unmarked grave. This was emphasised by my Mum's insistence in her later years that I make sure her burial money was available. That conversation was ongoing, with me always reassuring her. She died in 2008 here in Australia, and to complete her story, there was plenty of insurance money to give her a great farewell.

*   *   *

I have a huge love of fresh flowers.

As a child, they were such a big part of my life. My Grandma was one of the first flower-sellers of London, and they were recognised by dignitaries. They even had their own pew at the famous St Clement Danes Church at the Strand, and I believe to this day any descendant of these gorgeous women (as this work was always deemed a women's vocation) can get permission to marry at this beautiful church. I remember that every year women of a certain age would don their best bits, always with hats and gloves, and meet at the church to have a lovely day out. They travelled in a deluxe charabanc (a coach), heading to the coast for lunch like an Eliza Doolittle, but without the Rex Harrison.

What a glorious sight it was, as most of these women were really poverty stricken with very little education. They would buy bunches of flowers

– often violets – cheaply at Covent Garden flower market and make them into button holes and sell them to the toffs in the affluent West End of London. Many of these well-to-do gentlemen had their favourite flower-sellers and would buy a boutonniere for their lapels every day of the week for a penny or two.

My Nan was only 12 when she became a seller. It was the norm in those days for this work to be carried out by young children from huge families. It helped put food on the table, and more importantly, kept them from the dreaded workhouse.

She was also a very clever businesswoman and voracious reader of every newspaper and book she could get her hands on. In fact, with her intelligence, she would have given the famous World War II codebreakers at Bletchley Park a run for their money.

In later years my Nan and Grandfather opened their own flower shop in the East End, capitalising on the tradition of enormous funerals with elaborate flower decorations in very poor areas of London.

My Nan was a floral artiste of the highest degree,

and I would watch her make the most beautiful sculptures with flowers. I have seen full-size greyhounds, a bed, dice and numerous names and descriptions: 'Mum', 'Dad', 'Nan', 'Arthur', 'Charlie', 'Alfie', 'Albert', 'Bertha' and 'Victoria', all made to order. You really had to see it to believe it, and for the wealthier clients, I remember funeral directors arranging horses that could actually cry real tears.

In our family business, it was expected and non-negotiable that as soon as you could move your fingers you were working. Instead of an infant's rattle, you had a flower, stem and wire thrust into your hands.

The polystyrene that is used these days was unheard of then, so each wreath was firstly moss wired together, then every flower was stemmed and wired, a very time-consuming and exacting science. Once a set of instructions was given, you were on your way. In some cases, we would even dye white carnations blue or any other colour that was not available.

As the fruit and vegetables were bought for consumption, so was a bunch of flowers. They were as important as a loaf of bread for the poor, which seems so strange as I write this now.

I spent a lot of time in Covent Garden Flower and Fruit Market. My Mum would plait my hair before I went to bed so we could get up at 4am, long before school, and get to the market to buy the best flowers.

There was no 'Toy Story' in my day, so my treat for coming along was a cowboy (what Cockneys would call an egg and bacon roll) all washed down with a mug of hot, sweet tea.

Flowers are a luxury these days, but they were essential when I was growing up. Every week all the grandchildren could ask for whatever flowers they wanted for their bedroom, and to this day my love of fresh flowers has not waned.

So, it is a rather long-winded YES for flowers from me, the aroma and the beauty of them. I believe flowers give such a beautiful feeling to anyone.

*   *   *

My Dad, Alf Melvin, was an 18-stone, 18½ inch-neck bloke – a big man. A one-time professional fighter, he fought at Eaton Manor which was a hang-out of the notorious Kray Brothers, but that is another story for another time. He fought under the name of Alfie Jackson, and he was a huge, beautiful giant, one of three brothers.

He ran a shady game of 'crown and anchor', the 19th century dice game popular with sailors, and three-card tricks outside Walthamstow Greyhound track and some busy London train stations. I recommend you look them up online; those games seemed fun unless you lost your 'bugs bunny'.

I would watch him colour in a large piece of strong plastic cloth with four squares: a heart, a diamond, a spade and a club. He could throw any die; he taught me how to hold and throw two dice between my second and third fingers with the other die rattling round in a tin. He even cut the tin and put masking tape around the top, the idea being to make a big rattle with the one die whilst knowing what you were going to throw with the two dice between your fingers. I hasten to add my die-throwing training was only carried out in our own home for entertainment purposes.

All was going great. I imagined through my young eyes that I was much closer to my Dad's calm, smiling, laughing personality than to my Mum's strong and loud character, and growing up with this contrast gave me much love and safety. I was the apple of both my parents' eyes, in a house of security and fun.

The night that everything changed is etched into my memory. It was the night before my 12th birthday, and my Mum's 42nd birthday. It was the 28th of January 1963, when my beloved Dad died suddenly and tragically.

There is no sugar coating this, as difficult as it is to tell. My father took his own life with a gun in the Soho club that he operated, having shot and killed a man who owed him money. As it was explained to me – and it was in the newspapers as well – Dad demanded repayment from this man, a gangster named Tony Mella, who handed him a gun and dared him to make something of it.

His honour challenged, Dad responded by taking out Mella, and then turning the same gun on himself. It became known as the Bus Stop Murder.

As all old East End families do, they closed ranks. My Mum, her sister and three brothers and my Nan let nobody in. My Mum and I immediately moved into my Nan's house, where there were bedrooms on every floor. Mum's sister and Nan's were at the top and my Uncle and Aunt down below. Family was everywhere and the hatches were firmly battened down.

On hearing this tragic news my Mum screamed – and I mean screamed – for six weeks, non-stop. There seemed to be no end to her distress and at one point, she tried to take her own life by slashing her wrists. I didn't see her for three weeks as she was at the top of the house with my Nan and Aunt. I was at the bottom with another Aunt and Uncle. When she finally emerged, she did not recognise me.

My Mum had a complete breakdown, both physically and emotionally. She should have been committed to psychiatric care, but instead the family decided to have a doctor come every day and try to medicate her and help her function. The doctor did see me in passing and asked if I was okay. I answered, "yes", but that was the beginning and end of my grief therapy session.

As was the custom in those days, children were meant to be seen and not heard, but I felt like I was not even seen. I was not even allowed to attend

Dad's funeral, being farmed off to a distant family relative I hardly knew.

From that moment, I instinctively knew I must now be the parent and take care of my Mum so she would never get into that emotional state again. Overnight, I changed from a child to an adult.

I became terribly silent and introverted, as if watching this tragedy from afar. It was my first encounter with death and dying, and I remember thinking, "Is this what life is all about, did everybody go through this?"

Right up to my young adult life I felt this sequence of events had a profound effect on me. I never had proper closure after my father's death. I didn't see him die and didn't see his body afterward, nor did I have the chance to say goodbye at a funeral service. It was as though I had been tricked, and more than once I imagined I had seen my Dad walking down the street.

*   *   *

School for me was the Skinners Company School for girls, and it went as smoothly as it could. The tragedy did take a toll on me, though, and I moved from near the top of the class to further down the ranks in a very short space of time. No one seemed to notice, including me. However, this did not deter me from my thirst for knowledge, reading, life, and how to laugh in the face of adversity.

Further education passed me by but I did attend a finishing school. To the uninitiated, this meant that I learnt to walk around with a book on my head without it falling, riding side-saddle like the Queen, and being able to talk 'proper'.

After that, my early jobs ranged from market stall trading to modelling, merchandising, and some media work, but my biggest job remained managing my mother.

My boyfriends were few and far between, coming and going, as they failed to pass family security screening and the barrage of questions:

'Who's your mother? Who's your father? What do you know? Where do you live? What do you do for a living?'

Then came Robert Alan Shearer, better known as Bob, who I met at a tennis tournament in Bournemouth in the UK, where I had been working with Jackie Butterworth, now Jackie Newton. Jackie had only recently started dating the renowned Australian pro golfer of the 1970s, Jack Newton, whose career would be ended by a collision with an aeroplane propeller at a Sydney airport in 1983, severing his right arm.

Jack had invited along a few of his good mates from the European Golf Tour this particular night, for a party in a pub, in honour of Jackie. Jack asked me to have a dance with one of those friends, thinking that I would be good for Bob Shearer. Who knew? Maybe Jack did! That was May 1973. My first trip to Australia followed in December that year, our engagement to be married came in January, 1974 and the wedding in January, 1975

Bob passed the first test with my family simply by omission.

Nan: "Where do you live son?"

Bob: "Australia, Nan."

Nan: No answer with blank vacant look.

Nan (after some thought): "Who is your mother?"

Bob: "Murt and Les, Nan."

Nan: Blank vacant look, now with a watery smile followed by a silent pause.

Nan: "Who do you know?"

Bob: "Tony Jacklin, Arnold Palmer, Jack Nicklaus, Tom Watson, Ian Stanley, Jack Newton."

Nan: (Now with a puzzled face, no knowledge, no nod of head, immediate change of subject to the killer $6 million question): "What do you do for a living?"

Bob: (With the rest of the family leaning forward, inquisitively): "I play golf."

Silence prevailed, tongues were swallowed, eyes were crossed, sharp intakes of breath were heard, tumbleweed filled the room.

Everyone eagerly anticipated the next question, but none was forthcoming, as I sat in the corner silently. For the first time ever, it seemed, the family was lost for words en masse. Then, after what seemed like an eternity:

Nan: "No son, what is your JOB?"

Bob: "I play golf."

This totally confused everyone. Further discreet investigations were required. This was unfinished business.

Unfortunately, Bob's schedule meant that he sometimes had days off during the week and this was in the 1970s when the European Tour was in its infancy. My Nan, who spent a lot of time at our house, saw Bob often on his days off and this caused her great concern.

"No work today, son?" she repeatedly asked until my Mum devised a plan to put her at ease.

She told Nan that Bob was a member of the Australian Armed Services and in peace time, did not have to be on duty often. This was never confirmed or denied.

After my grandmother died and we were able to put to sleep Vice Admiral Shearer, my family reinvented themselves as golf fans. Lyle and Scott V-neck Argyle sweaters became the norm, along with three-button golf shirts, check pants and Tam O'shanter hats. We all discovered Jack Nicklaus was not a brand of shoes but in fact a champion player, perhaps the best ever, and that Arnold Palmer did not make umbrellas, but in reality was one of the most famous golfers in the world who happened to use that particular implement for personal branding.

Leather seats or 'shooting sticks' were now always carried in the trunk of cars. As soon as pro-ams or tournaments could be attended, the family drove to golf courses, especially to Scotland. What a colourful lot we all were – clubhouse tickets were a must, and the everyday vocabulary now included expressions like pin-high, bogeys and birdies.

After our marriage we lived in the United States for eight years playing on the US Tour. It amounted to being on the road for 30 weeks a year.

Bob was a fine player. He went on to win 27 professional tournaments, including the 1983 Australian PGA Championship at Royal Melbourne Golf Club, and the 1982 Australian Open at The Australian Golf Club in Sydney, where he went down the stretch with no less a figure than the great Nicklaus. He had two wins on the European Tour, one on the US Tour, and spent many years playing the European Senior Tour where he won numerous times. He became a life member of the Australian PGA.

During our time in America, we had two lovely lads, Bobby and Brett, who both live and work in Melbourne.

Bobby spent some time caddying for Bob on the senior tour. Later he took up landscape gardening, moved down to the Mornington Peninsula, and gave Bob and I our only grandchild, Jake Jackson, named after my Dad. Brett has had the same job as a storeman for a fantastic family for the past 15 years and still lives at home.

They are compassionate and kind boys. We all think our ducks are swans, but in my case, I love them, and I love the way they think.

*   *   *

Bob stood back from the main US tour in the mid-1980s following a few health scares, and decided that he wanted to return home to Melbourne.

The next major change in my life came in 1989, when Bob played a round of golf with the very respected Australian golfer, Graham Marsh, who had played a lot in Japan and was about to bring a big tournament to Australia, the Coca-Cola Classic to be played at Royal Melbourne. He asked Bob if I would be interested in taking a role, as my previous working experience included event management and coordination.

Bob came home, very pleased with himself to say that he had not only found me a job, but I would be starting immediately. He told me to drop everything, failing to consider the implications of raising two young lads, 11 and 7 years respectively, plus the washing, ironing, shopping and house management. I was very concerned about this, but I kept that to myself.

At the tournament I was allocated to look after Media Management which turned out to be the start of a 30-year love affair.

This media work was seasonal, but I did travel overseas to Europe, Asia and the US. Now I found that I could run a home, work hard away from home and still take care of the family. My ingrained work ethic came to the fore, and in my down time, I learned that I could still fit in a few more bits and pieces.

Studying to be a celebrant for weddings – and in particular funerals – was always something that I had fancied. All through my life this subject intrigued me; I saw it as 'speaking for someone who didn't have a voice'. What an honour that would be, I felt.

Along with my friend and colleague, Julie Lockhart, I embarked on a celebrants' course which would allow me to hatch, match and dispatch members of the human race.

It is this circle of life that inspired me to start the process of writing this book. So many times in this new job, I saw families unprepared, stricken by grief and not knowing how to manage the death of a loved one.

Concerns over costs were often not considered. Families often equated money with how much they loved the departed. Morally, ethically, I know there must be another way. I am certainly not saying funeral companies are not needed. My goodness, they are vital, but it is my obligation to let you know there are some choices.

'Get up, dress up and show up.'
– Bette Melvin, my mother

Notes

2. THE LIGHTBULB MOMENT

'Shine a light on me.'

was on a trip overseas in Spain in the winter of 2008 when I had a revelation. My Mother Bette was in assisted living accommodation, and while I saw her six days a week she would phone me 12 times a day on my one day off from visiting her.

The trip was part of a twice-a-year ritual of mine, of meeting with a group of friends from the United States, Denmark and the United Kingdom. We were all at different stages of our lives, some with teenage children, some with elderly parents, some single, some married.

My close friend Dorthe Galli was among them, and Dorthe would research those trips to make them fun and interesting for everyone. I would be away from my Melbourne home for a maximum of three weeks.

Bob and my lads would take it in turns to visit Mum, with a schedule written up to ensure that she always had a visitor. I would even record messages before I left, saying, "Good morning, Mum, up you get now."

She was in the very early stages of what I might politely call 'OldTimers'.

Off I went overseas, believing all was in place. A very generous friend gave me his Frequent Flyer Points which allowed me to travel and enjoy business class. Oh, the bliss of the service and big wide seats, away from life and reality.

The only issue was that I had to travel around the world to get anywhere, not strictly a problem for me as I loved and love the non-contactable environment of those big metal containers.

The break was fantastic – a birthday party in Puerto Banus in Spain, a trip to the Alhambra in Granada, some walking, talking, eating and of course the odd tipple or two.

Every couple of days I contacted home to see

if my Mum was okay and that everything was on schedule. Visitors were dropping in to see her until the point when I started my journey home.

It was Saturday morning and I would be home on the Monday as my ticket would take me from Spain to Amsterdam, on to Japan where I had to overnight stay, before heading to Brisbane, then into Melbourne. I felt like Phileas Fogg, around the world in three days rather than 80! I can honestly say I was looking forward to every part of the journey. Champagne, mimosa cocktails and relentless look-a-like caviar and frozen cake. Those were the days my friend. However, I digress.

I spoke to Bob on Saturday morning from Spain, when all of my friends had left to go back to their lives around the world. I was on my own, and as usual, my question to Bob was, "How is Bette?" He answered, "Not well."

That said everything really, and just like that, as Sarah Jessica Parker said, everything changed.

Bob told me that my dear Mother, a gorgeous, large woman, had ceased three of her favourite pastimes – eating, drinking and talking. My journey home took on a new meaning.

My first stop was Amsterdam, and the connection was tight, so I could do nothing until I got to Japan. My luggage was lost in transit meaning that I had to stay overnight. Australia seemed far, far away, I was totally uncontactable and I felt so very much on my own. I had to come to terms with not seeing my Mum alive again, with only my own thoughts for company.

My Mum was 86 years old and had always refused to discuss her parting. I never slept a wink, spending every moment wondering what I could do as I tried to get home to Melbourne to see her before she died.

As it happened, I did manage to find my way home to see Mum on the last day of her life. In the next few chapters of *Last Orders*, I will share how I came to the realisation of what a brilliant gift my Mum had left.

We live in a culture that likes to pretend the most obvious things are not real if they are the slightest bit unpleasant. Most people avoid talking about dying, as it can be very confronting, scary and very painful.

My Mum's death taught me we need not hide our heads in the sand. It planted a seed in my confused brain box. Imagine if everything was sorted in people's lives before they died. They could live their lives knowing everything was set up for when they can no longer speak for themselves.

I, for one, have booked my holiday: my seat is confirmed, my bags are packed, and my passport is ready for life everlasting. The details are ready for my family to follow. I want them to remember me in a loving way, I want to make them smile when someone speaks of me, to laugh when someone repeats a crazy story and I want them to say my name without sadness.

Notes

'Oh wow, oh wow, oh wow!'

Last words: Steve Jobs, co-founder of Apple

3. PLANNING FOR YOUR DESTINATION UNKNOWN

'I am no longer on the road to nowhere.'

There have been several times in my life when I have felt that I was on the road to nowhere. After my Dad passed away, there was absolutely nothing in place. No will, no arrangements, and why would there have been in 1963? There was nothing to prepare anybody back then. It was customary that the local undertaker took over every step of the process with no questions asked, and no one knew anything different.

By the time my Mum died 45 years later I was prepared – so much so that 18 months earlier my younger son, Brett, a budding filmmaker, recorded a piece asking my Mum about her life story. He cut it down to a 17-minute monologue which I played at her funeral.

Even with the best preparation, you are never prepared for the reality of this moment. Fortunately, as an only child, my Mum had the good sense to give me complete autonomy over her affairs.

At face value, outsiders assumed everything was okay, but handling this situation on my own was a very lonely place at times. I remember thinking, "If only my twin were still here to share this burden."

This can also be a time when the most harmonious of families begin to fracture, as everyone has different ideas about what should be happening, as well as the wants and desires of the lost one.

For example, at the celebration of a couple of close friends, one had an estranged son that he never acknowledged due to family conflict. Another, a forceful man, who thought he should speak at his brother's funeral after not actually having much contact in the later years. Both events caused terrible distress at a most difficult time.

My goodness, what a gift it would have been if *Last Orders* had been on hand.

Let me share what I feel should be in place, so

you can raise that glass of champagne or beer, with a smile. From this point forward you are commencing your Last Orders journey in earnest.

In most western countries, legal authority over a loved one's life if they become incapacitated (whether relating to wealth and/or health) is called an Enduring Power of Attorney.

The wealth aspect will consider how your money will be spent, taking into account your day-to-day expenses and potential care. Of course, if you are close to your children, they are the perfect people to relay your wishes. I suggest choosing children or much younger people, rather than your partner, as youth is an advantage at this stage. You need someone who will outlive you, if possible.

If you don't have good connections with your family, I suggest handing the reins to a trusted friend.

The health aspect is a very touchy subject that none of us want to address, as it can be much more emotionally complicated. You will need to consider a power of attorney involving this person very carefully. Imagine you are on a life support machine and it has to be turned off. What a decision that would be.

A friend had a niece who was in a car accident. She was a healthy, beautiful and much-loved 21-year-old, who drove into a tree and ended up in a coma. There was no power of attorney, and as a result, the life support machine could not be turned off due to her age. The whole family then took care of her, visiting and sitting with her every day for an agonising and distressing seven long years.

The hospital said she had no brain function, so she had effectively died on the night of the accident. Within those seven years, her mother died of cancer. Her grandfather died as well. The family still believes the stress caused all of this. The whole family fractured. Privately, time and time again, they wished someone had had the authority to say enough is enough.

Other areas needing careful consideration are what would happen if you were to drop off the perch unexpectedly or were to contract a terminal illness.

Sudden death is exactly what happened to my husband in 2022. Bob was 72, and did not appear to be ill. Yes, he was a diabetic and had a defibrillator implant in his body, yet he still played golf three times a week in his golf cart. The night that he died, he had watched Cameron Smith winning a PGA Tour event in Hawaii.

It was 9 January 2022, the day before our 46th wedding anniversary when he collapsed at home.

I called the emergency services, and a lovely man came alone, followed by two young policewomen. They declared that he could not be resuscitated. Foul play had been ruled out, but neither party was keen to take away Bob's body. I showed the paramedic Bob's pills and insulin, and he said that he felt comfortable to release the body and the policewomen agreed, so they left Bob on the floor in the bedroom.

Thank goodness I knew what my next call would be. It was to the cremation company (who I had already researched) who came within the hour and took Bob away. By that time my two sons, a cousin, and great friends had all arrived at our home, and they were able to say goodbye.

When someone close to you dies, there are financial and other decisions to be made. As an only child, I did them all for my Mum and as Bob's wife, I had to do it again.

As soon as I got the death certificate, I photocopied it 10 times as I knew it needed to be certified. This allowed me to deal with the banks, the insurance company, the superannuation company and the pay-TV provider to name but a few. It seemed to go on for months, with no short cuts. Even two years later, the bank was still sending me letters addressed to the Bob Shearer Estate. Frustrating!

'Goodbye kid, hurry back.'
Last words: Humphrey Bogart to Lauren Bacall

Notes

4. WHERE THERE'S A
WILL, THERE'S A WAY

'Signed sealed delivered, I'm yours' (or if you are really lucky)… 'Money, Money, Money.'

Before going into the details of looking at your estate, I want to say again that I totally believe in having a fabulous life. My ethos is having control over your destiny, enjoying your life and planning to minimise the bother of your passing for others.

Having things prepared means someone else can make decisions quickly and easily with minimal stress.

A great place to begin is by having an awareness

of your worth and, more importantly, what you value. What you are worth and what you value are key to being able to decide where you want it all to go when you have departed this earth.

Once you know what you have, you could plan all sorts of fun activities, meeting aspirations and ticking off the old bucket list while you are alive, and even enjoy it with others. Then (if you want) you can have the cheapest send-off possible.

Obviously in financial terms, the best (but alas, impossible) scenario would be to know when you are going to die and work backwards. This would mean you could do everything you ever wanted to do (within reason) and plan to the last penny how much you will need before the final curtain comes down.

A long time ago I came to the conclusion that your hard-earned money is for enjoyment, but soon realised that this concept means different things to different people. Ultimately, it's up to you.

Now, to the will – the document that sets out how to distribute your estate.

The majority of people do not want to approach writing a will. They regard it as morbid. They delude themselves into thinking that their death is so far in the future that it's not worth worrying about for the time being. In other words, many of us never get around to it.

So many people act as though death will never happen to them.

There must be an assumption that those we leave behind will know exactly what to do and how to implement our wishes.

More often than not, they do not know, so you need to make it clear while you can.

I will define exactly what I mean by a will.

The definition used in most western countries (and this may change from place to place) is: 'A will, or testament is a legal document by which a person, the testator, expresses their wishes as to how their property is to be distributed at death, and names one or more persons, the executor, to manage the estate until its final distribution'.

In broad terms this means: Who do you want to give your money to? Do you have a named person(s), legal representative or organisation who will make this happen? We are assuming you have money left because, as I have said previously, hopefully the majority will be gone as you will have enjoyed yourself!

How you would like your wishes carried out is another thing altogether. It could be a document associated with your will, and this is where you have to be very clear what you want.

A friend said to me recently that she would like something said at her celebration, and my response was: "Where is it written?" To which there was a silence, and my next statement was clear. "Please write it down!"

The type of requests involved in this document are things like: 'Where I want to be buried', or 'What happens to my body after I die', or 'What I'd like said about me' and 'What music to play at my funeral'.

In Melbourne, a retired solicitor, David Whiting, has for many years provided free legal advice on ABC radio. I have been an avid listener. People call in with questions, and it is quite enlightening. I am always amazed how many disagreements there are in this space, especially relating to estates and wills.

One in particular that Whiting dealt with concerned a mature lady who wanted to leave all her money to a wildlife sanctuary. She stated that she had given her two sons a wonderful education, she felt they were beautifully set up and she had done enough and they did not need her money. Whiting replied: "Did they say they didn't want your money, or are you assuming that?" She said the conversation had not taken place, and that her sons knew nothing of her wishes.

Whiting was succinct, "Well, you had better give it all away before you die, because wills can be contested and we all know where money is concerned, personalities can sometimes change."

Some people go to amazing extremes. There is the story of the lumber millionaire Wellington R Burt, who died in 1919 in the United States but held back his enormous fortune until 21 years after his last surviving grandchild died. The money sat in trust for all of 92 years until 2011.

The consequences of not having a will are dire, to be frank. I was reminded recently of the Sydney businessman Andrew Findlay, who did not pen a will and who died in 2023. His family is fighting it out over the $20 million estate in court, with all the dirty linen being aired in public hearings. What a terrible waste of time and money from which only the lawyers will benefit.

So who ya gonna call? Ghostbusters? I don't think so.

When you decide to make a will, you need to contact a solicitor.

An important part of the process is to have an executor who will keep a cool and steady hand on your affairs, otherwise it will be left for the courts to sort out your life savings and possessions and all that hard earned cash could be whittled away in fees. If all else fails, you can appoint a public trustee for a fee.

My own will and that of my two boys are held by a local solicitor in Mentone, Melbourne, but if you feel your estate is straight-forward then a post office or newsagent will be able to supply a template. Note that you will need a witness.

I also recommend a booklet put out by Centrelink in Australia, entitled 'When Someone Dies', which has an excellent list of people and places you can contact in your time of need. The link is at the back of this book.

'Will you still love me tomorrow' – The Shirelles say it beautifully.

Your will is one of the most important documents you will ever produce. Without one, you are asking for aggravation as money, money, money can be the root of all evil and frankly, it makes people do the strangest things. It could turn Doris Day into Morticia from the Addams Family.

As part of the Last Orders family we will be producing an aid which will give you some pointers on recording information.

It will cover many topics and give you useful tips:

- About You
- Your Money
- Your Property
- Your Possessions
- Your Celebration
- Your Wishes

The message is clear: having a will is one of the most important things you can do to make your passage to the afterlife smoother for those you leave behind. Fail to get it done, and there is a world of trouble that you have inflicted upon your loved ones.

'Are you happy? I am happy.'
Last words: Ethel Merman,
Broadway musical theatre star

Notes

5. THE YUKKY BIT – WHAT DO I DO WITH MY BODY?

'Dem bones, dem bones, dem dry bones.'

The first thing to remember about this subject is that this is your body and you can do with it what you want, even if in some instances the people left behind may not agree with your decision.

I will bet that you have never thought about what happens to your body (that is, your flesh and bones) once your spirit or soul or life blood (or however you want to explain it) has left your mortal remains.

The majority of people assume that this is just taken care of. Some people are happy to assume that it will all be okay because of their religious beliefs, and that is totally fine, too. But what if you had choices? Would you consider things differently? Because surprise, surprise! There are choices and those choices belong only to you.

I know that sounds simplistic, but I suppose we have to consider many other things when deciding what to do with our bodies – such as how the people left behind would handle your choice, and somehow bringing proper closure to your life.

We now hope to explore these choices so you can make informed decisions.

I suspect the majority of us know of only two ways of body disposal that we have ever discussed – these being burial or cremation. Even these two alternatives have many permutations, and that is usually the beginning and end of the subject, However in reality, there are so many alternatives.

As food for thought, you can certainly leave your body for medical science, pre-arranged so that someone will pick up your body, use it for research, then return your ashes to the family.

Other alternatives for consideration include:
- Natural burial in woodland
- Buried at sea

- Remains in a rock
- Cryogenics (waiting for a cure, ask Walt Disney)
- Remains going into outer space

The list goes on ...

Then you might have to consider what receptacle you wish your ashes or body to be placed in. There are many, but to name a few:

- Wicker basket
- Wool casket
- Cardboard (you might want to consider supplying pens so a message can be written)
- Self-designed casket
- Body bag (at sea)

Again, the list goes on......

You can of course be buried with all the trimmings and a number of religions prefer this.

My mother and Bob were cremated. I had tried on many occasions to open the subject with my mother, whose sister and brother-in-law followed her over to Australia from the UK.

They lived so close by they could wave to one another from their lounge rooms – literally across the road. Unfortunately, my Mum's younger sister died before her, and her headstone now sits next to her husband in Bunurong Memorial Park in Melbourne, a huge and lovely cemetery not too far from where we all lived.

I offered to buy my Mum the plot next door to her sister and brother-in-law. She was so affronted with my suggestion it became a running joke in the family. She relayed this story, and without drawing a breath replied, "Not yet! Are you trying to get rid of me?"

I must add at this stage she was 83 years old, not very mobile and still harboured a desire to return to Las Vegas which we had all visited a number of years earlier, bringing out Mum's love of the nightlife. She never made it back to Las Vegas and she never did get a stone next to beloved sister and brother-in-law.

Instead, some of her ashes are at the City of London cemetery with my Dad with a new stone – together again. I was left with the remaining ashes. I wanted to keep them in Australia, but had no headstone to take them to. Secretly, I was really pleased, as after my father died in 1963, every Sunday, no matter how bad the elements were, we would make our way to the cemetery, armed with the most beautiful bunches of chrysanthemums. Pots were emptied, water refilled, old flowers thrown away and fingers frozen. There were always tears from my Mum, and I became quite fascinated with the other tombstones. In my child's eyes, those visits went on for years, and certainly I believe that we never missed a Sunday for the first year.

Back in Australia, I had my Mum's ashes sitting in a beautiful velvet box in my lounge for the next few years. Still thinking about where I might spread them, I would enquire what everyone else did with their loved one's ashes, and it amazed me that we were all looking for a perfect place. One close friend told me that she kept her husband's ashes in the boot of their Mercedes car. Another kept her son's ashes under the bed.

Others stored them in urns – reminding me of the hilarious scene in the movie Meet the Parents, where Ben Stiller's character, in popping a bottle of champagne, accidentally upends the urn containing the ashes of his prospective father-in-law's (played by Robert de Niro) mother, sending them all over the floor for the cat to fossick in.

Mum's ashes sat in the lounge for a number of years without me finding an answer to the quandary. I knew of her love of flowers and the garden, so eventually I thought: 'What would be the best way to join those together in the best place?' Then like a thunderbolt it hit me! Why not have the ashes contained in the garden?

I researched this but soon enough found that there was nothing available for burying ashes in a garden other than for pets. So I went to work and designed my own rock which fitted the container that held Mum's ashes – a rock that would accommodate the standard funeral receptacle. I tweaked the design to incorporate a memorial plaque, and Bette now sits proudly in the garden. Fondly admired, that rock is fully transportable and will come with me wherever I move in the future.

There is also embalming, a funeral practice that's been carried out for thousands of years. In some parts of the world, extreme embalming has seen people temporarily preserved to be photographed with family members, or put on display.

There is no obligation or need to embalm your

loved one. Embalming a body is optional, and it has a cost.

So why do people embalm a body?

People look different after death. Embalming can help restore the person's appearance, giving an impression of peaceful sleep and wellness. Some people want to have the body on display in an open coffin at home, or in a church or a chapel of rest, and prefer an embalmed body to do this.

If you do opt for embalming, typically the funeral directors will embalm the body, wash the person's body, set their features including stitching their face in a particular style, brush their hair and dress them and put them on display in a chapel. The body is kept refrigerated between viewings.

It can take between eight and 12 years for an unembalmed body, buried six feet down, to decompose to a skeleton. An embalmed body may take longer to decompose. An embalmed body can take many years to fully decompose (depending on the environment). Concrete-lined graves or burial vaults may slow the process further, and in the right conditions, embalming fluids can preserve a body indefinitely.

What happens with your body is your choice to make, and you should go ahead and make it. Communicating that decision will be one of the greatest gifts that you can leave your family.

'Time for another drink.'
Last words: Jack Daniels, founder of Jack
Daniel's Tennessee Whiskey

Notes

6. MY SEND-OFF, WITH ALL THE TRIMMINGS

'It's my party and I'll cry if I want to.'

This is always a very sensitive subject, and I preface this by saying I have worked with many funeral directors, from the very expensive – and I mean expensive – to the very modest.

I was surprised to learn that most funeral homes are owned by a few companies, although I have come across a few family-owned companies, but they are few and far between.

As we all know, it can be a time of great distress, and sometimes we are led to believe that if we spend a lot of money on our dearly departed it shows to everyone how loved they are, how respected they were, what an important part they had in our family.

I am here to say that love does not equate to the amount of money you spend on a funeral.

We are sometimes persuaded that if we don't give our departed a frilly pillow to lay their head on, they will somehow be less comfortable.

My own Dad had a pale blue ruffled pillow but, as a celebrant, I have viewed a lot of bodies that have passed on to life everlasting, and surprisingly, they have never whispered to me that their pillow was uncomfortable and asked if I could change it for them.

I had a friend who had a piper play at his Mum's funeral. She was not Scottish, and had no connections with Scotland, but he was convinced that she would have liked it, and that she deserved it. More expense.

I gave my own mother a great send-off, quite inexpensively. I did a number of things the funeral director tried to tell me I could not do.

Of course, I tried to discuss with my Mum her wishes while she was still alive. However, getting her to discuss anything around this subject was like pulling teeth as she believed she was not going to die anytime soon.

I remember when we once broached the taboo subject, she said: 'I want a big funeral with lots of flowers (remembering our background as florists in London) and with lots of people there." The first was no problem; the second, I was not sure that I could promise.

I did try to explain to her that she was 86 and had already been in her 60s when she migrated. We are a small family, me being the only living child, all of her sisters and brothers had died and we did not belong to a club of any kind, so how were we going to draw a big crowd?

For the last six months of her life Mum did not even know where she was (other than knowing that she wanted to go back to Las Vegas).

My husband Bob's celebration was arranged at his spiritual home, the Southern Golf Club. About 300 people attended with live screen tributes from many of his friends and playing partners as well as being Zoomed around the word for those who were unable to attend.

A most wonderful bronze statue by Louis

Laumen now stands proudly at Southern, near the first tee with Bob in full swing with a golf club in hand. Some of his ashes are beneath that statue with the rest at home in the garden in his own 'Love in a Rock' where I can come and have a natter with him from time to time.

Cost was not too much of a factor for both the celebrations of my beloved Mum and Bob.

I know how terribly lucky I was in both cases that my experience as a celebrant gave me a few useful tips.

I cannot begin to tell you how the exorbitant costs of giving a loved one a respectful send-off truly disturb me.

Let's start at the end and go backwards – which is really what this book is trying to address – before your last hurrah.

More and more people are deciding to have a living funeral with friends and family, so they can enjoy it as well. Seeing as you are paying for it, you might as well join in! I love a good party. After all, 'it's my party and I'll cry if I want to'.

Living funerals can be accompanied by assisted euthanasia at a later date. It is fundamentally a way of saying goodbye.

Although this may seem strange, I have been to a couple of these occasions, and in fact, at what is a terribly sad time, it can be quite cathartic. It can certainly leave you melancholy for some time afterwards, but the long-term memories can make you smile.

Don't get me wrong, funeral companies certainly have their place. However, in times of grief we often are not in the right head space to make the clearest decisions. We often don't have all of the facts and figures, and in the moment, we don't care and we are very vulnerable.

I played it differently for my Mum when she died.

I decided reluctantly cremation was the way to go. I already had the name of the company I wanted to use, one I trusted and had recommended dozens of times in my job. It's a wonderful young company that I feel complete satisfaction with. So I picked up my Mum's ashes two weeks after she was cremated, allowing plenty of time to think and sort out what was a good send-off for her ... without the piper of course!

As I mentioned earlier, my son had recorded and

edited a little piece of a living diary of my Mum's life, and I found an appropriate funeral home to arrange a chapel. I started the service by saying:

'Welcome, now let my Mum, who always had a lot to say, speak for herself!'

Her face came up on two big video screens. Her first words were:

'If you are watching this, then it means I am on my way to life everlasting'.

She spoke for 17 minutes. We played the Boogie Woogie Bugle Boy by the Andrews sisters, John Denver's Some Days Are Diamonds, and finished with Patsy Cline's Crazy.

I ended by saying, 'She made me crazy, I loved her like crazy, and I will miss her like crazy!'

I printed the order of service myself on gorgeous paper and bought two lovely guest books from the local stationers for people to sign. Roses from the local grower bloomed out loud, and then it was all back to my house for a great BBQ, sausage rolls, party pies, champagne, wine and beer with the celebrations going into the early hours. My Mum's ashes were on full display.

When the dust settled and I had a chance to

reflect on the event, it gave me a great deal of satisfaction and relief, knowing that I did the best that I could.

If you want to explore how I did things in a bit more detail I have developed an easy-to-follow tutorial, which covers every other aspect of dying happy.

These are the questions that you ask yourself in these moments.

The idea is: to make it easier for everyone. We're not reinventing the wheel here. It's about providing the information and the resources so you understand and can implement the right options for you.

'Am I dying or is this my birthday?'
Last words: Lady Nancy Astor, first woman
seated Member of UK Parliament

Notes

7. PERCEPTION OR REALITY: HOW DO I SEE ME? HOW DO OTHERS SEE ME?

'Knowing Me, Knowing You, A-Ha.'

This is the opportunity to talk about ourselves, which can be a challenge for some of us.

Inevitably when I conduct funeral ceremonies I will do some research in collaboration with families so that a eulogy can be prepared.

It never ceases to amaze me how many unknown facts come to light. Even within the tightest family there are so many stories that are lost in the mists of time, as people's memories fade and the older generations die off.

A great singer, a brilliant tennis player, a diligent

charity worker, a community representative and even some comical facts they would rather forget – these things do come out.

How many beers they could drink in one session dancing on tables, the list can go on. Not forgetting how many memories are uncovered at the after-ceremony meeting wherever that may be.

So here is my point: imagine if that was all known before, so that family and friends could hear and laugh together.

In an ideal world, we pass away with nothing left unsaid. You can do this by various means: perhaps compile a eulogy, write a book, film a video. You can write a note or letter to your loved ones, which some people do, and perhaps leave it to be opened after you have gone.

Others like to include a little secret meant to be unveiled after their passing, although one needs to be aware of possible fall-out and impact on others.

More often it might be some kind of message that the departing person hopes will be helpful, comforting, even funny for those who are left behind.

Ideally you would record information during

your life and add it to your departing message as you go along.

A video is a great idea, easy to do and very effective. My mother's video tells me that. It can be done professionally, or with a loved one's mobile phone and can have a lasting impact for your loved ones.

In my mother's case it took the form of an interview, but it could just as easily have been a monologue. This could be a general message to all your family or if required, to specific people. Remember that we don't want anything left unsaid. That is the key point.

*'I've had a hell of a lot of fun and
have enjoyed every minute.'*
Last words: Errol Flynn, famous actor
from the Golden Age of Hollywood

Notes

NEARLY FINISHED...

'Almost there.'

– Andy Williams

Phew! If you have reached this page in the book – well done!

I hope I haven't bored you – pardon the pun – to death. I have written this book – in part – as a love letter to my family, and I have been eager to share this with you before I went totally round the twist.

This is my aide memoire, leaving enough gaps for you to fill in whatever you feel is appropriate to assist you with your journey.

I have covered some hard topics. In my case, my lads know that I want a cremation, a party consisting of Costco sandwiches, sushi, wine and beer, and not forgetting lovely roses.

Music will consist of The Carnival is Over, Phil Collins following up with A Groovy Kind of Love and James Taylor sending me to sleep … and everyone else for that matter! I have my playlist ready and waiting with tunes like Yesterday, Here Comes The Sun by the London Philharmonic Orchestra, Might As Well Dance by Madeline Perzut, Throw Your Arms Around Me by Mark Seymour and a few others from Tracy Chapman, Ed Sheeran and Luke Coombs.

My ashes are to be placed in my very own 'Love in a Rock' in the garden – the lads could even split my ashes if they wish.

Although this was not meant to be a self-help book for me, I have to say it did throw up a lot of emotions and memories which I thought I had forgotten. I never doubted my memory, however I thought long and hard and sometimes and doubted that my life was worth including in such detail in *Last Orders*.

I hope this book will make you smile, laugh and perhaps cry – all at the same time. I have always found that life can be so very beautiful. I learnt that no one knows what is in store for us when we leave this mortal world, but I hope whoever we leave behind that has loved us is left with a sense of understanding and peace.

I hope that by reading *Last Orders*, you'll have left no song unsung. I trust by sharing this with you, I will have assisted you at a difficult and complicated time in your life.

This book has become a huge part of me and my life. It was never meant to be that way – in fact it has been much more difficult that I could have imagined.

My beautiful journey with my sons Bobby and Brett and my grandson Jake – along with countless other family members, friends, neighbours, colleagues and associates too numerous to name – has allowed me, with this wonderfully random brain of mine, to shape these words into some kind of order. It has truly been a labour of love, filled with laughter, longing, smiles and sadness, and sprinkled with a few tears.

It was never meant to be War and Peace, more a little nudge for us all to contemplate our future.

Maybe it has touched a nerve and made you think of things differently. You may even just write one or two things down.

I have one lovely friend, Ian, who said to me: 'I am just going to leave it up for my family to sort out'.

Which is absolutely fine if it has already been discussed. If *Last Orders* has made you think about things, then writing this book would've been totally worth it for me.

For now cheerio until the next book!

Love and peace always, from 'Kaffie the almost Aussie' Shearer.

'It is beautiful.'
Last words: Elizabeth Barrett Browning,
Victorian English poet

Notes

MY TO-DO LIST

'Zip-a-Dee-Doo-Dah!'

Now that you've reached the point of taking real action, your mind is likely filled with questions, tasks and plans. Let's take a moment to pause and simplify things.

I've created the following list to help you begin preparing your own Last Orders. These basic steps will guide you through the key things to consider, so you can move forward with clarity and peace of mind. When the time comes, you'll be ready to leave this life with a sense of completion and a smile.

Remember, this is a living document. It should grow and evolve with you, and be reviewed regularly, especially after major life changes. So, let's get started:

1. Make a will and let your loved ones know where it is.

2. Think about how you would like to be farewelled, and go into whatever level of detail you desire. Give explicit instructions so that your loved ones are not left guessing. If you are being cremated, for instance, indicate where your ashes should be spread or kept. If you are being buried, buy a plot. Write everything down and put your wishes in a place where your loved ones can find them.

3. Record or write down a message or more than one if you like. Again, the level of detail is up to you, but a video works well. You might want to compile a little life story so that your memories are not erased when you depart. Work on the basis that nothing should be left unsaid.

4. Review your wishes regularly. Things can change, and there is no reason why you cannot revise your plan.

'Tape Seinfeld for me.'
Last words: Harvey Korman,
American actor and comedian

Notes

CONCLUSION –
NOW THIS IS THE END

This book is fundamentally a call to action.

I'm here to make you think.

I don't want to lecture people.

But I wrote *Last Orders* because I have seen too many people who reach the end of their lives, with no clue how to handle it.

Twenty-two years as a celebrant, and longer than that in the school of life, tells me that around 80 percent of people either die or lose a loved one with no idea what they want for the farewell.

Then, of course, grieving family and friends are expected to pick up the slack and make decisions when they are in no state to do so. They are exhausted and they are vulnerable.

It can get worse. Divisions appear within families and old wounds are opened. I have seen people adopt a completely different personality under the pressure of extreme grief. In these situations, a united family can disintegrate. A loving sister suddenly becomes an enemy sibling.

Why? Because they don't know what to do, and in most of our cultures, they have precious little time to make the decisions that they are being asked to make in just a few days.

Even when there is a long lead-up to a person's death, for instance if they are terminally ill, and possibly in palliative care, people are reluctant to ask the questions they need to ask.

And then the regret comes. *Why didn't I ask him/ her?*

It's utterly maddening, and I don't want to see it.

I advocate a small but precise piece of planning for the ultimate end so that a life can be celebrated with less stress about what comes after. It's not difficult to decide if you want to be buried or cremated, and it's easy to make a will. It's not hard to leave strong guidelines for your funeral or service.

It takes only a few minutes to write letters to your children, as I have, to have a video interview prepared, as we did with my mother. If you have a grievance that has been left simmering, perhaps that can be addressed in a note.

Practical matters can be dealt with. Bank account locations and numbers, and the bane of everyone's life – passwords and PINs.

If you have a will, and it is imperative that you do, make sure that its location is well known. The same would apply to a power of attorney. Perhaps have your documents stored with a solicitor, or otherwise with a trusted friend.

As I have said, I look upon it as though you are planning a fabulous cruise. You pay beforehand, and order the full drinks menu so that you can enjoy yourself. I've done it myself, and I know that it gives you a sense of calm, relief and peace.

Why did I write this book and why does it matter? Because I want to help people. I want to show them a different way.

For your loved ones, if you create some sort of

document and make sure that they know exactly where it is, it will be the best gift that you can give them.

You will have your own ideas, no doubt. But here's a little plan, as an example of what you can do and what to consider:

Articulate your wishes for:
1. Any significant other
2. Partner/spouse
3. Children
4. Friends

Use simple words:
1. Love
2. Apologies
3. Practical things that they need to know

My Will information:
1. Will location
2. My financial power of attorney
3. My medical power of attorney

Other Documents:

1. Financial information
2. Bank address/account number
3. Credit Card
4. Investment account
5. Retirement account
6. Loans
7. Safety deposit boxes
8. Bills to be paid
9. Property
10. Family trusts
11. Login information
12. Online accounts
13. Important downloads
14. Life insurance
15. Car insurance
16. Superannuation

Ask how these documents can be safely stored:

1. Safety deposit boxes
2. On the cloud storage
3. Life binder
4. Fireproof box

My friends, I advise you to take your own advice on these matters as well. The suggestions that I have made come from 20-plus years of experience, yet I would never pretend that they cover everything or that they are perfect.

What I wanted was to be thought-provoking.

If I had made you think, then I'm glad. That was my whole point from the first word.

We have the potential to do something very special. To turn a beautiful life into a beautiful death as well.

Although there is so much more that can be added to the conclusion in this book, i.e. marriage lines, legal information documents, mortgages and legals, I feel that I can only advise that this will make life so much easier for your nearest and dearest – however, you may want to keep these details to yourself. They are so important but also so private – perhaps you can put them in a sealed envelope, with a note as to where they can be found, in a locked box, with your bank or with a solicitor, that is for you and only you to decide.

Just as a side line I know in my family, my grandmother Jane Bromley/Jane Eveniss/Jane

Hooper, born 1891 was not married until after her five children were born. Shock horror when her marriage lines were found in an old handbag, after she passed away, she decided to tell anyone and good on her!

'Remember honey, don't forget what I told you.
Put in my coffin a deck of cards , a golf club
and a pretty blonde.'
Last words: Chico Marx,
American actor and comedian

Notes

ACKNOWLEDGMENTS

'Thank you for the music.'

Once again, I want to give a huge thank you to my son Brett, who so beautifully transcribed my random and almost indecipherable handwritten scribbles.

To Mike and Debby Clayton, for their deep knowledge of me and their tireless editing of scores of haphazard words (and sometimes outright drivel) - I'm incredibly grateful.

To my cousin Martin and his partner Jeffrey (who brought the peace), thank you for all the shouting, laughter, frustration, patience, and above all, love.

To Martin Blake and his calm, steady partner Fi - thank you.

To my publisher Graeme Ryan and book designer Luke Harris – thank you both for your patience especially with all the toing and froing and countless changes.

And finally, to everyone else I may have missed, far too many to mention – thank you as well.

Fondest always,

Kathie Shearer

USEFUL LINKS AND RESOURCES

Beyond Blue:

beyondblue.org.au

Services Australia:

servicesaustralia.gov.au/
who-to-tell-when-someone-dies?context=60101

Lifeline:

lifeline.org.au

Reporting a death:

deathnotification.gov.au

Notes

LOVE IN A ROCK

Now that you've read this book, I hope it has encouraged you to see this subject from a fresh, or at least slightly different, perspective.

Drawing from my own experiences, and as part of the Last Orders family of services, I've created **Love in a Rock** – a handmade, portable memorial that holds a loved one's ashes. It enables you to keep your loved one close – whether in your garden, on a terrace or balcony, or even inside your home.

With the spiralling cost of funerals, saying goodbye in a meaningful yet affordable way can be difficult. Love in a Rock offers a thoughtful alternative to traditional burials and memorials, helping you avoid cemetery, headstone and maintenance costs – while still keeping your loved one with you, always.

If you'd like more information or advice, please visit **loveinarock.com** or email me at bigloveinarock@gmail.com.

A LIFE PRESERVED FOREVER

D o you want your life story told in book form? Is it your desire to put your anecdotes and tales down on paper for posterity, so that your kids and grandkids remember them?

So many people go to their graves and take the storytelling with them.

The editor of this book and a part of the Last Orders team, lifelong journalist Martin Blake, is an experienced 'ghost' writer of autobiographies as well as having pieced together the life stories of many people. The process is simple and painless and only takes a few months.

But the result lasts forever.

To contact Martin for a quote,

email him: martinjblake61@gmail.com

Notes

www.ingramcontent.com/pod-product-compliance
Lightning Source LLC
Chambersburg PA
CBHW021342090426
42742CB00008B/700